W9-CET-742

CATS Are Better Than MEN

BECAUSE...

You can "fix" your cat.

Cats are clean. They cover up their own mess.

CATS Are Better Than MEN Because...

Written by
Donna Hanbery
and the Cucumber Group

Illustrated by
Martin Riskin

IVORY TOWER PUBLISHING COMPANY INCORPORATED

COPYRIGHT 1993

NO PORTION OF THIS BOOK MAY BE REPRODUCED MECHANICALLY OR ELECTRONICALLY OR BY ANY OTHER MEANS INCLUDING PHOTOCOPYING WITHOUT THE PERMISSION OF THE PUBLISHER.

MADE IN THE U.S.A.

PUBLISHED SIMULTANEOUSLY IN CANADA BY MARKA CANADA ETOBICOKE, ONTARIO M9W 5Z6

DISTRIBUTED IN AUSTRALIA BY SKANSEN SYDNEY

DISTRIBUTED IN THE UNITED KINGDOM BY

ANYTHING GOES SURBITON, SURREY KT6 7RL

DISTRIBUTED IN NEW ZEALAND BY BLACKWOOD GAYLE DISTRIBUTORS AUCKLAND.

2 3 4 5 6 7 8 9 10
11 12 13 14 15 16 17 18
19 20 21 22 23 24 25
26 27 28 29 30

IVORY TOWER PUBLISHING COMPANY, INC.
125 WALNUT ST., P.O. BOX 9132
WATERTOWN, MA 02272-9132
TEL#: (617) 923-1111
FAX: (617) 923-8839

BECAUSE...

A cat won't criticize your taste in movies. A cat won't wise off if you cry during "An Affair to Remember," "Love Story" or "The Way We Were."

CATS ARE BETTER THAN MEN

BECAUSE...

With a cat, you control the remote. A cat will never expect you to watch "All Star Wrestling" or the "Game of the Week" every day of the week.

A cat will never tell you to "be quiet" until halftime.

Cats are purr-fect companions. A cat is willing
to keep you company while you're sewing, cooking,
cleaning or reading.

Cats are trustworthy. A cat will never do
sneaky things behind your back.

It doesn't hurt when a cat walks all over you.

CATS Are Better Than MEN

BECAUSE...

You can live with more than one cat at a time.

Cats aren't embarrassed to show affection in public.

A cat will never call you from jail, a bar at closing time or another woman's house.

Cats love to bring you presents.

Cats are compact. You don't have to be a contortionist
to share a twin bed, couch or chair with a cat.

Cats think food out of cans is great!

CATS ARE Better Than MEN

BECAUSE...

Cats are always home for the holidays. Cats are always eager to help trim the tree.

CATS Are Better Than MEN

BECAUSE...

A fat cat is still adorable.

CATS ARE BETTER THAN MEN

BECAUSE...

Cats still look good when they're old and gray.

A cat will never complain if you hog the bathroom.

CATS ARE Better Than MEN

BECAUSE...

Cats are not afraid to make a commitment
that involves a few risks.

Cats won't snicker when they watch you try on clothes.

Cats are entertaining. Cats can be amusing without using four letter words, sexual innuendoes or putting women down.

Cats are easily excited. The mere sight of a bird
can send a cat into ecstasy.

CATS ARE BETTER THAN MEN

BECAUSE...

It doesn't hurt your feelings if your cat sleeps around.

A cat will never expect you to get rid of your boyfriend because "it's allergic."

CATS ARE Better Than MEN

BECAUSE...

Cats are silent sleepers. They don't snore, wheeze or talk in their sleep.

You'll never feel guilty because you slept with a cat.

Cats think you are fascinating. Cats are curious about everything you do.

CATS ARE Better Than MEN

BECAUSE....

Good grooming is important to cats. Cats never go a day without cleaning, and they even wash all those hard to reach places.

Cats enjoy the little things in life. Squirrels, birds, butterflies and bugs can make your cat's day.

Cats may play "hard to get" but they don't really mean it.

BECAUSE...

Cats like to get their own dinner (usually off the counter, table or shelves that you were sure they couldn't reach.)

You can drop a cat and it will still land on its feet.
A cat will never sue you for alimony, palimony
or joint custody of the kittens.

CATS Are Better Than MEN

BECAUSE...

Cats don't pout if you have to stay late at work.
They're always glad to see you when you come home.
Cats are never threatened by your job.

CATS ARE BETTER THAN MEN

BECAUSE...

Cats have refined dining habits.
It's more appetizing to watch a cat eat a mouse than to
watch any man drink at a bar.

It's easy to share a bathroom with a cat.
A cat will never complain about your bathroom habits.
Cats are good company during bubble baths.

It's inexpensive to travel with a cat. Cats fly free.

A cat will never insist on driving <u>your</u> car. A cat will never borrow your car on full, return it on empty, with the seat pushed back and your radio buttons all reprogrammed.

A cat will never fill up your living room
with its sports equipment.

CATS ARE BETTER THAN MEN

BECAUSE...

A cat will never expect you to wear kinky lingerie around the house. To a feline, that old bathrobe and flannel is the cat's pajamas.

You'll never have to choose between your cat
and your career. A cat won't refuse to move when
a promotion requires a transfer.

BECAUSE...

Cats like you just the way you are. A cat doesn't expect you to improve yourself. A cat would never sign you up for aerobic classes.

Cats understand when you get PMS.

Cats aren't into sports. A cat will never expect you to
come to its games or go into mourning
when its team loses.

A cat won't eat you out of house and home
and send you out for more groceries.

IVORY TOWER PUBLISHING COMPANY INCORPORATED

125 Walnut Street, P.O. Box 9132, Watertown, MA 02272-9132

These other fun books are available at many fine stores or by sending $3.50 ea. directly to the publisher plus shipping.

2026-Games You Can Play In Bed. A humorous compendium covering everything from Bedtime Bingo to Things To Do at 3:45 A.M.

2034-You Know You're Over 40 When... You Think "Grass" is something to cut and "Getting a little action" means your prune juice is working. A perfect 40th birthday gift.

2042-Cucumbers Are Better Than Men Because... They don't care if you shave your legs and they never walk around your place when the shades are up. At last, ladies, revenge for all our male chauvinist books.

2064-The Wedding Night - Facing Nuptial Terrors. For brides and grooms alike: What To Do If He Wants To Take Pictures; What To Do If She Won't Come Out Of The Bathroom; and many more hilariously funny situations newlyweds may encounter.

2067-It's Time To Retire When... Your boss is younger than you are, you stop to think and sometimes forget to start again, or you feel like the morning after and you swear you haven't been anywhere.

2068-Sex Manual For People Over 30. Includes great excuses for non-performance, rediscovering foreplay, and how to tell an orgasm from a heart attack.

2102-You Know You're Over 50 When... You add "God willing" to the end of most of your statements and you don't care where your wife goes when she goes out, as long as you don't have to go with her. A great 50-year-old birthday gift.

2109-The Get Well Book. Cheer up sick folks with this book that teaches them how to gain sympathy, what the doctor really means and how to cope with phones, kids, germs and critters that make you sick.

2127-Your Golf Game Is In Big Trouble When... Your practice rounds are all in the bar, you've tried out 30 putters and none of them work and you play whole rounds without once hitting the fairway.

2131-The Fart Book. Farts are divided into two groups. 1. Your farts. 2. Somebody else's fart. This book lists them all, the Little Girls Don't Fart Fart, The Dog Did It Fart, the S'cuse Me Fart and many more.

2136-The Shit List. The list is quite extensive and describes the versatile use of this clever word. There is, for example, "chicken shit" and "give a shit" and "shoot the shit". A very funny book, No Shit.

2148-Dear Teacher...A hilarious collection of actual parents' notes to teachers. "Please excuse Joe from school yesterday. He had diarrhea through a hole in his shoe."

2166-You've Survived Catholic School When... You can enter a phone booth without feeling you should begin confessing and you don't shudder when someone hands you a ruler.

2177-You're Over the Hill When... No one cares anymore about what you did in high school and you see your old cereal bowl in an antique shop.

2190-Teddy Bears Are Better Than Men Because... They don't hog the whole bed and they invariably understand when you have a headache.

2192-You Know You're Over 30 When... You start wearing underwear almost all of the time, you find the first grey hair and you no longer have to lie on your resume.

2195-Beer Is Better Than Women Because... Beers don't want a lasting relationship and beer doesn't expect an hour of foreplay before satisfying you.

2198-The P.M.S. Book. What every woman experiences once a month. Includes the Irritability Syndrome, the Tender Boobs Syndrome and the Chocolate Syndrome.

2203-The Last Fart Book. This final sequel concludes with the Under The Cover Fart, the Waiting Room Fart, the Excuses Fart and many others.

2205-Is There Sex After 40? Normal 40-year-olds do it once a week. Covers everything from sexy cardigans to tucking a T-shirt into your underpants.

2210- Is There Sex After Marriage? This great work covers everything from faking an orgasm to philandering to excuses for more or less sex. It even answers the old question, Is There Sex After Pets?

2213- Women Over 50 Are Better... They can tune out the worst snoring, have more womanly figures & won't make you sleep in the middle of a stuffed animal collection.

2216-Hanky Panky. Cartoons of the animal kingdom in their favorite amorous (and unmentionable) pastime. Brilliant full color drawings are riotously funny.

2217-Is There Sex After 50? Swapping your mate for two 25-year-olds, finding places to put your cold feet, and telling grandchildren about when you were a hippy.

2224-Life's A Picnic If You Have A Big Weenie. Covers where big weenies come from, what women like about big weenies, making a teenie weenie into a big weenie, and much more.

2225-Women Over 40 Are Better Because... They know just what it takes to make their man feel good and they can eat a double hot fudge sundae and not worry about "breaking out".

2226-C.R.S. (Can't Remember Shit). It happens to the best of us like forgetting the punch line of a great joke, where you parked the car, or where you left your glasses.

2227-Happy Birthday! You Know You're A Year Older When... You no longer eat all the dessert just because it's there and you can no longer easily sleep till noon.

2228-You're Hooked On Fishing When... You start to raise your own worms, you visit the emergency room at least once a year to have a hook removed, and you're on a first name basis with the Coast Guard.

2229-You Know You're A Redneck When... You wear bib overalls, eat grits, love cow tipping, and think a mud wrestling place is hog heaven.

2230-A Coloring Book for Pregnant Mothers To Be. Tender and funny, from being unable to see the scale to controlling your proud parents.

2231-Eating Pussy The Official Cat Cookbook. This book will not only offer you great new ideas for serving pussy to your guests, but it is sure to expand your recipe file.

2232-Life's More Fun When You're 21... This book humorously covers the trials of coming of age such as parental trust, joining the work force, and balancing budgets.

2233-Small Busted Women Are Better Because. Finally a book that boasts the benefits of being small busted in our society where bigger is better! A super way to bolster the ego of every slender woman.

2234-You Know You're Over 60 When... You're 60 when you start straddling two road lanes, you start looking forward to dull evenings at home, and you can't remember when prunes and figs weren't a regular part of your diet.

2235-You Know You're Over 70 When... You have trouble sleeping, though you're an expert at napping and you carry enough antacid pills to get any group through any meal.

2236-The Nose Picker's Guide. Learn everything there is to know about what comes out of your nose, from all the different types to the many ways to dispose of them.

2237-55 & Picking Up Speed. There is no stopping the growth of hair in your ears & nose; you leave programming the VCR to people under 25.

2239-The Working Woman's Guide to the Male Organ. A detailed guide of men who own WeeWees, Members, Weenies, Schlongs, Tools, and many others. Everyone is covered, from accountants to taxi drivers.

2240-Dumb Men Jokes. Why are all dumb blond jokes one liners? — So men can understand them. A real revenge book for women everywhere.

TRADE BOOKS - $7.00 Postpaid

2400-How To Have Sex On Your Birthday. Finding a partner, special birthday sex positions, places to keep your birthday erection, faking the birthday orgasm and much more.

2402-Confessions From The Bathroom. The Gas Station Dump, for example, the Porta Pottie Dump, the Sunday Newspaper Dump to mention just a few.

2403-The Good Bonking Guide. Bonking is a great new British term for doing "you know what". Covers bonking in the dark, bonking all night long, improving your bonking and everything else you've ever wanted (or maybe didn't want) to know.

2407-40 Happens. You realize anyone with the energy to do it on a weeknight must be a sex maniac.

2408-30 Happens. You take out a lifetime membership at your health club and you still wonder when the baby fat will finally disappear.

2409-50 Happens. When you can't remember what you went to the top of the stairs for and when "made in Japan" meant something that didn't work.

2411-Geriatric Sex Guide. It's not his mind that needs expanding and you're in the mood now, but by the time you're naked, you won't be!

2412-Golf Shots. Humorously tells you how to look for lost balls, what excuses to use to play through first, ways to distract your opponent, and where and when a true golfer is willing to play golf.

2414-60 Happens. When your kids start to look middle-aged and when your hearing is perfect if everyone would just stop mumbling.

2416-The Absolutely Worst Fart Book. What is The Absolutely Worst Fart? Is it the First Date Fart, The Oh My God Don't Let Me Fart Now Fart, The Doctor's Exam Fart? There are many, many choices. You choose.

2417-Women Over 30 Are Better... Their nightmares about exams are starting to fade and their handbags can sustain life for about a week with no outside support whatsoever.

2418-9 Months In The Sac. A humorous look at pregnancy through the eyes of the baby, such as: why do pregnant women have to go to the bathroom as soon as they get to the store?

2419-Cucumbers Are Better Than Men... (Part II). Cucumbers are always ready when you are and cucumbers will never hear "yes, yes" when you're saying "NO, NO."

2421-Honeymoon Guide. Every IMPORTANT thing to know about the honeymoon—from The Advantages Of Undressing With The Light On (it's slightly easier to undo a bra) to What Men Want Most (being allowed to sleep right afterwards without having to talk about love).

2422-Eat Yourself Healthy. Calories only add up if the food is consumed at a table. Snacking and stand up nibbling don't count. Green M&M's are full of the same vitamins found in broccoli and lots of other useful eating information your mother never told you.

2423-Is There Sex After 40? Your wife liked you better when the bulge above your waist used to be the bulge in your trousers. You think wife-swapping means getting someone else to cook for you.

2424-Is There Sex After 50? Going to bed early just means a chance to catch up on your reading or watch a little extra t.v., and you find that you actually miss trying to make love quietly so as not to wake the children.

2425-Women Over 40 Are Better... Over 90 reasons why women over 40 really are better: They realize that no matter how many sit-ups and leg raises they do, they cannot recapture their 17-year-old figures, but they find something attractive in any 21-year-old guy.

2426-Women Over 50 Are Better... More reasons why women over 50 are better: They will be amused if you take them parking, and they know that being alone is better than being with someone they don't like.

2427-You're Over The Hill When... All the stories of your youth have already bored most acquaintances several times over. Even worse, you've resigned to being slightly overweight after trying every diet that has come along in the last 15 years.

2428-Beer Is Better Than Women... (Part II). A beer doesn't get upset if you call it by the wrong name; and after several beers, you can roll over to sleep without having to talk about love.

2429-Married To A Computer. You're married to a computer if you fondle it daily, you keep in touch when you're travelling and you stare at it a lot without understanding it. You even eat most meals with it.

2430-Is There Sex After 30? Parking isn't as much fun as it was in high school. He thinks foreplay means parading around nude in front of the mirror, holding his stomach in; and she knows the quickest way to get rid of an unwanted date is to talk about commitment.

2431-Happy Birthday You Old Fart! You're an Old Fart when you spend less and less time between visits to a toilet, your back goes out more than you do, and you tend to refer to anyone under 40 as a "kid."

2432-Big Weenies. Why some people have big weenies while other people have teenie weenies; rating a weenie; as well as the kinds of men who possess a putz, a prong, a member, a rod and a wang—and more!

2433-Games You Can Play With Your Pussy. Why everyone should have a pussy; how to give a pussy a bath (grease the sides of the tub so it won't be able to claw its way out); and more!

2434-Sex And Marriage. What wives want out of marriage (romance, respect and a Bloomingdale's Charge Card); what husbands want out of marriage (to be left alone when watching football games and to be allowed to go to sleep after sex).